LOVE Me this WAY

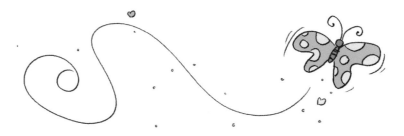

Written by **Lee Ellen Aven**
Illustrated by **Anil Tortop**
Designed by **Ozan Tortop**
ISBN: 978-0-9887846-0-4

Dedicated to
the creative passionate
flame of life
within each of us.

Everyone has a child within from Day 1 until the last day.

It is the voice that directs our passions and our creative expression.

We all want to be encouraged, clearly heard and fully recognized every step along the way.

Here is the way...

When I am around you,
keep a smile in your heart.
That way...
I will always know you appreciate me
for who I AM.

I will see this
in the twinkle of your eyes
and
I will feel it
because you will want to give me
at least one hug.

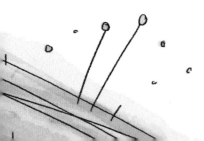

On my birthday,
say to me:
"I am SO glad you were born!"
and hopefully... you will mean it.
But,
even if you don't,
it will make me feel special just to hear this from you.

When I give you a present,
tell me:
"I REALLY like it!"
even if you don't
really.

When I tell you:
"I have an idea!"
please be *EXCITED*.
And ask me:
"What's your idea?"
And DO tell me how great it is that I am having ideas.

But,
DO NOT tell me about your ideas just then. Wait 'til later.

At least once a day,
share with me what makes you happy.
This will give me permission to find things
that make me happy and share them with you.
Then I won't think it's MY job to make YOU happy.
What a relief.

And,
please **listen carefully**
when I tell you what makes me happy
so you will always know
what to give me for my birthday.

Also,
I like when you remember my favorite food
and you make it for me every once in a while.
And mostly...
I like when you say all that out loud.

When I am sad,
please
let me be sad.
But,
make sure you hold me close most of the time
when I'm sad
until I tell you I'm okay.

When I tell you:
"I'M SCARED!"
What I really want is for you to make me feel safe.
Never tell me NOT to be scared because
it's too late for that -
I'M ALREADY SCARED!

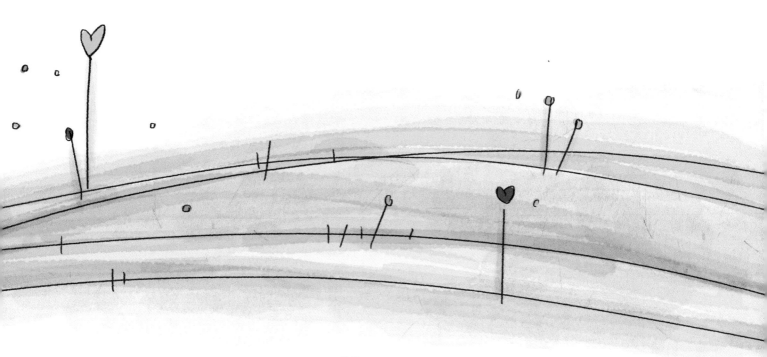

Here are ways to make me feel safe:

1) Wrap your arms all the way around me
and tell me you will always be there
no matter what.
2) Look me straight in the eye and say:
"You are safe
I am here"
and really mean it.

That is the deal we made when you agreed to love me.

When I show you that I'm not feeling like my happy, *sparkly* self, and I have many ways to show you that...
Please – instead of being impatient and upset with me and so sure that you can tell me how to get happy again – I need you to reach deep into your kindness bag to pull out an imaginary blanket lined with understanding and patience
to *GENTLY* wrap around me until I feel better.

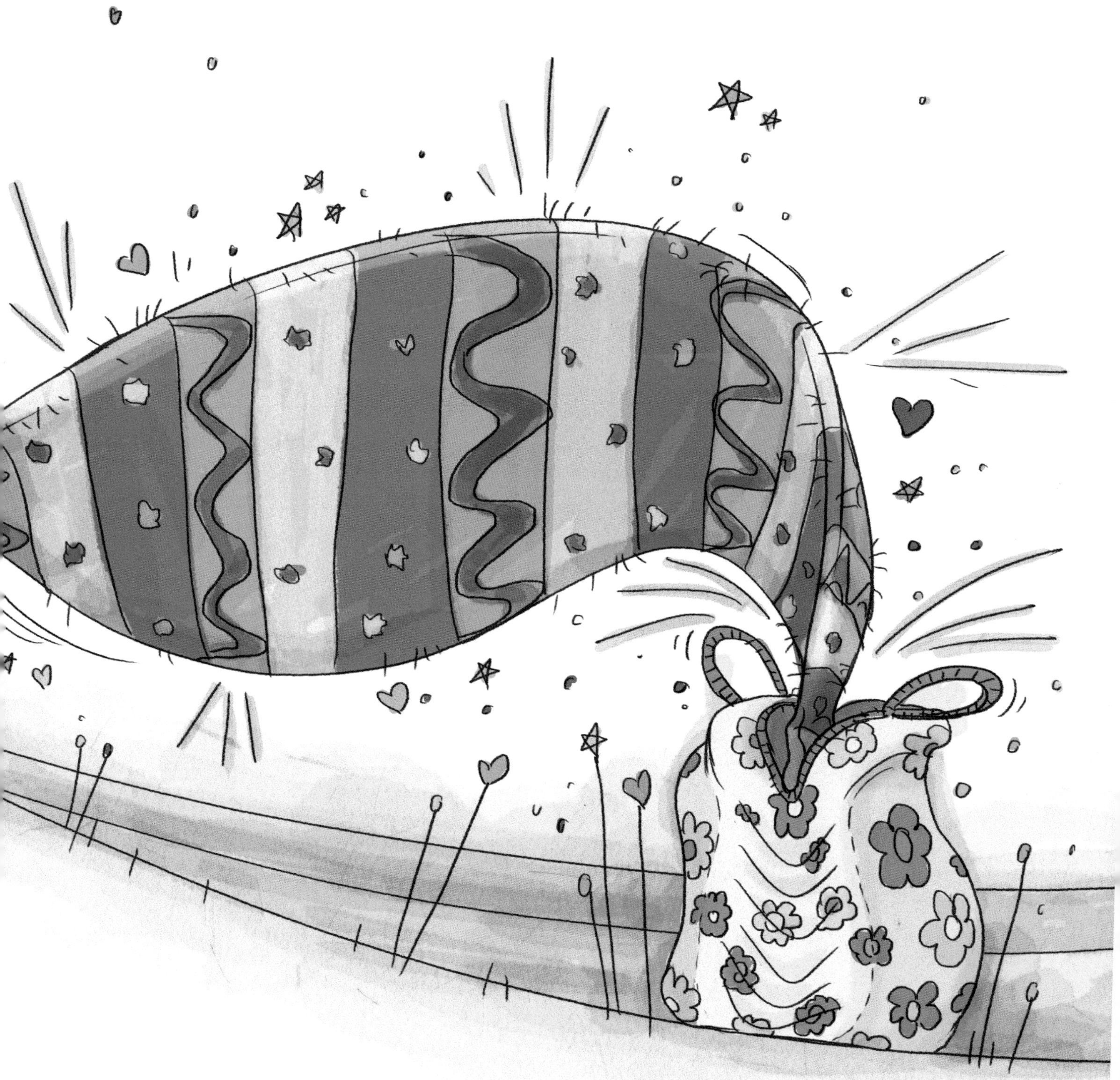

When it gets easier for me,
you will know
IF
you pay attention.

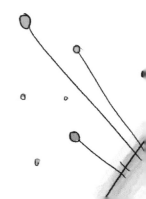

Sorry,
but I won't really care how YOU are feeling just then.
I will be much too distracted by my own situation
and that is quite enough for me.
My request for you would be
to magically grow wings to fly above your situation
so you can be *forgiving* toward me
and know that I am okay
even if I am uncomfortable while trying to figure things out.

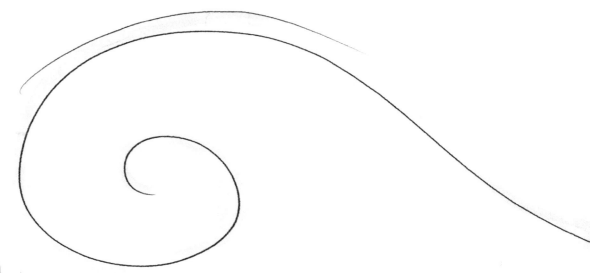

And then
there are the times when it IS right that my behavior
distresses you...

Did I get a bit too creative in bending the rules?

Did I do something that wasn't safe?

Was I not paying attention when I should have been?

Well,
you can be disappointed
even very disappointed
or very, very disappointed
but *please* don't be so angry.

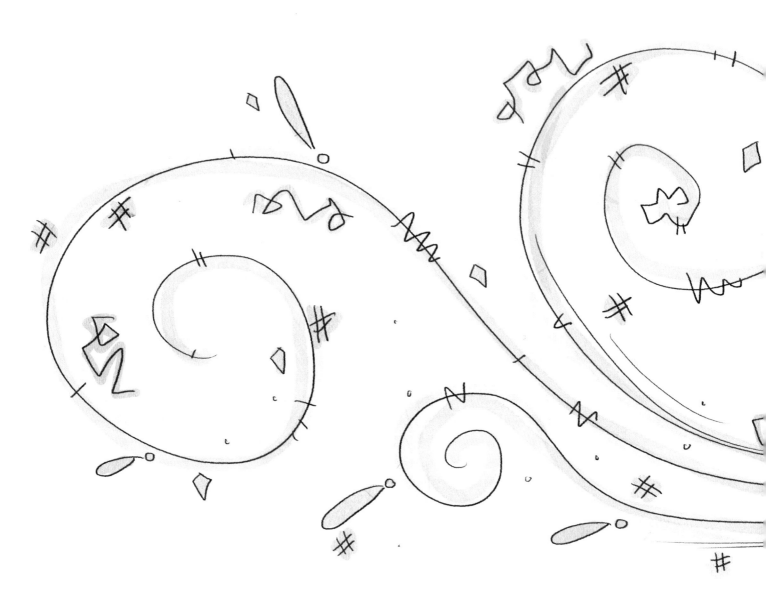

Try **REALLY** hard
to breathe out most of your anger
before
you say one word to me.

You can be strict or stern
but still be nice to me
with your heart
if you know what I mean.

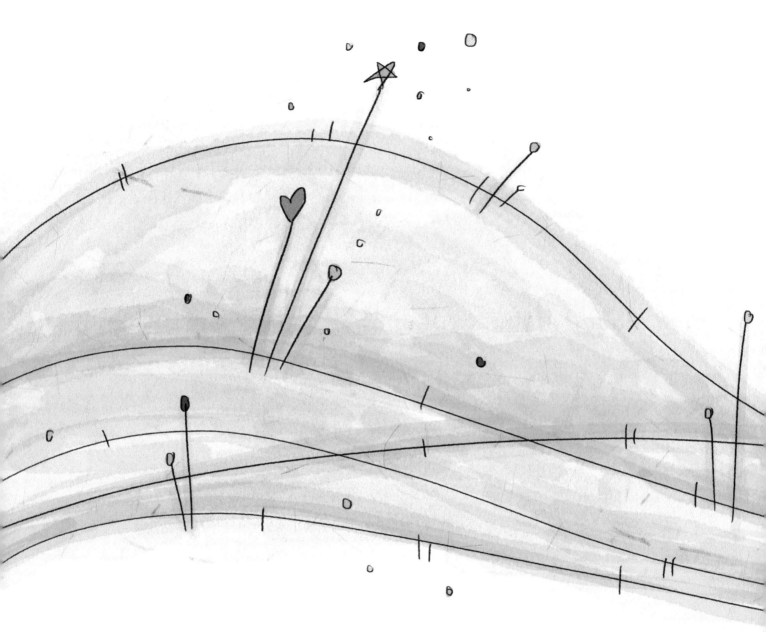

Because sometimes
life just happens
and you do want me to stay eager for more!

All that I have shared with you here is
important to know
but,
if there is one thing
you are to remember and one thing only -

HERE IT IS -

THE MOST IMPORTANT OF ALL...

Always see
what's good and strong about me
(even if you have to pretend)
and
if you *tell* me
what's good and strong about me
and
tell me often...

I PROMISE

it will **always** be true.

-the end-

LEE AVEN

Born with a fascination for what makes people tick, Lee has been a people watcher forever. As a daughter, a mother, a sister, a friend, as an RN working with families in early intervention, as a nutritionist at the Martha's Vineyard Hospital - all the while honing skills as an energy medicine worker, she is continually observing the magical positive effects that personal validation has on everyone every time.
lovemethiswaybook.com

ANIL TORTOP

Anil was born and grew up in Turkey. Besides being the illustrator of more than 30 children's books, she is also an animator. The world of children is her greatest inspiration. Since 2010 she's been trying to get used to Australian semi-wild life and unstable weather.
aniltortop.com - tadaabook.com

ACKNOWLEDGEMENTS

Thank you to my two amazing children for continually teaching me and making me always reach deeper within to understand about individuality and creative juices. Thank you to my husband for his comic relief, his everlasting love and support and for asking me years ago, "How's your book coming?" even before I knew it was coming. Hugs to my labradoodle for being my constant loyal companion. Thank you to my friends who love me unconditionally and to my family for their caring. My gratitude for the teachings of Abraham, as brought to us through Esther and Jerry Hicks and for the teachings of Deborah King, Wayne Dyer and Louise Hay. And blessings to my extraordinary illustrator and design team, Anil and Ozan from TadaaBook, for making my vision a reality even while residing on the opposite end of the earth.

17616079R00025

Made in the USA
Charleston, SC
20 February 2013